questions for the dead

poems

k.b. marie

This book is a product of the author's imagination. Any references to historical events, real people, or real places have been used fictitiously. Other names, characters, places, and incidents are also the product of the author's imagination. Any resemblance to actual persons, living or dead, business establishments, events, or locales is entirely coincidental.

No part of this book shall be reproduced or transmitted in any form or by any means without prior written permission of the publisher. Although every precaution has been taken in preparation of the book, the publisher and the author assume no responsibility for errors or omissions. Neither is any liability assumed for damages resulting from the use of information contained in this book or its misuse.

Copyright © 2020 K.B. Marie
Illustrations by Victoria Solomon
Formatting by Jasie Gale
All rights reserved.

ISBN-13: 978-1-949577-34-1
ISBN-10: 1-949577-34-1

questions for the dead

table of contents

dedication
preface

woman playing the lute   11

I.
picture postcard of a kansas baptism   15
judith slaying holofernes again   19
on florentine art   20
annunciation II-IV   21
the convent of san marco   27
ode to a fellow writer in notebooks   28
the young martyr   29
little medieval boxes   30
parable of the lost   31
joan of arc   32
the artist's studio   34
ode to the unnamed   36

II.
the seasons   41
6 beauties of the pleasure quarter   43
the beggars   45
the raft of medusa   46
on stone   49
the dance of zalongo   50
the coronation   51

the burning of troy	52
in the tomb of donatello	53
michelangelo's tomb	55
hercules fighting the centaurs	56
the sacrifice	57
judith and her maid servant	58
the battlefield of eylau	60

III.

the medici chapels	65
mary magdalene	67
questions for the dead	69
emergence – or ode to the unfinished work	71
hercules at the crossroads	79
a final question	80
transmutation	81
les nymphéas	82
portrait of mrs. pagliano bruno	90

author's note
also by k.b. marie
about the author
about the illustrator

*This book is dedicated to all the artists in the world—
that means you.*

preface

A few years after completing my MFA, I was fortunate enough to have the opportunity to go to Europe for seven weeks. I had a single ambition for my time there: to write a collection of ekphrastic poetry.

If you're unfamiliar with the term ekphrastic poetry, The Poetry Foundation defines it as "a vivid description of a scene, or more commonly, a work of art" (Poetry Foundation).

This can mean poems about a particular work of art, or about the artist who created it. Sometimes it explores the problems of creation altogether. Many of my poems here do one of the three.

In order to achieve this goal, I split my time between Paris and Florence, two European cities in possession of large quantities of art.

Both were beautiful and perfectly safe for a woman traveling alone, but there was so much to take in—and distract—that I had a hard time imagining that my abundant scribblings were amounting to anything. It wasn't until I got home and was able to process the multitude of journals I had accumulated, that I was able to gain a sense of the collection emerging.

This is that collection.

I think ekphrastic poems are best enjoyed if the reader can look at the art that inspired them while also reading or listening to the poem. Most of what inspired me can be viewed by open resources on the internet or directly on the museum's website. To make your search easier, I often gave my poem the same title (or subtitle) as the artwork so you can find it for yourself.

While this method is not required to enjoy the collection this way—with both poem and art hand-in-hand—it is recommended.

In combining the two, I hope it opens up something inside you, that large resonant feeling I cherish so much. A connection to all the other human beings—past, present, and future—trying to make sense of this big, messy experience called *life*.

                                               woman playing the lute
                                                                 bega

The room has fallen down around you.
That is as it should be.

How can one see the world without
when watching the world within?

I've yet to master this duplicity myself.
The more I tune my compass,

the more I align with the unseen, the unreal,
the more unaware I am

of the books, the papers, the rules
slipping precariously over the table's edge.

At such times, it's easy to forget the sands
in the upturned hourglass are nearly spent.

The room is getting dark. The hour late.
And somewhere in this house a cold bed waits.

For now, I know only that I am lost, listening,
for the music that will lead me home.

I.

picture postcard of a kansas baptism
john steuart curry

1.

A woman dressed
in white is nearly lowered

into a basin of dirty water.
Her eyes are half-closed,

half-turned
up to the sky, watching

one white, one black dove
circle there. The people, forty bodies,

circle the basin. They're dressed
in Sunday's best. They sing.

The children look bored,
except for the one afraid of water.

Everyone is waiting,
even the house.

The house, empty, looks nervous.
The horse, tied, is ready to run.

2.

The man in black slacks
waits, holds the woman in white

but never lowers her into the water.
The widow looks smug beneath her veil—

I particularly dislike this look the widow gives
the woman in white, as if she knows

just what awaits a woman, submerged.
I care only for this woman in white,

arms resigned over her chest.
She is waiting. She is listening

for the voice—
There is no voice.

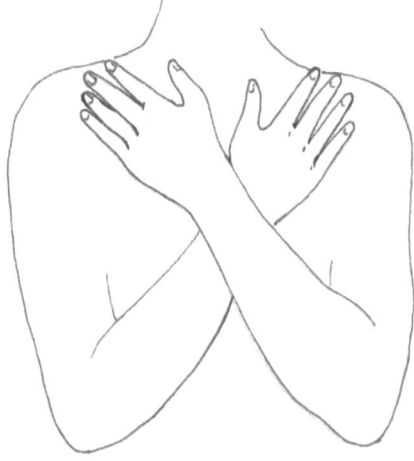

3.

Each of these stone mausoleums have names.
I enter: the Louvre at seventeen, the Uffizi at thirty-one.

I enter, leave, enter, leave, and cold
pillars make doorways. White softens all.

My face searches for what I need, and make no mistake,
we each need something.

I'm waiting for a voice, listening for
something that may never come. Yet, I see it everywhere—

in the black smudge of an oiled mouth,
in light caught, brush-stroked cheeks—

in the shadow of downcast eyes. All these tricks of
light, and here I can believe almost anything. Here,

I can hear departing footsteps echo in a great hall
and mistake its sound for someone speaking.

judith slaying holofernes again
artemisia gentileschi

How many times did you see it
in your mind before you put it down?
How many efforts to trace

the trapezoids, turning the bodies over
again in the light, again in the darkness?
Was it premonitory when you painted

Judith's face the first time?
Tassi must've been but a sketch
on a distant horizon, a silhouette

stretched long by the breaking
dawn. Then flesh made the horror real.
You gave her *more* the second time.

More muscle in the arms.
More focus in the eyes.
Was it that hard to overcome him?

Or that hard to overcome yourself?

on florentine art

You're scaring me. Everyone here is
so fond of gold, silver, marble, stone—

my choice of paper and pen, so vulnerable,
feels doomed to failure.

Chaucer, sure. Shakespeare, even better.
But I'm no great master.

I've no loyal disciples to carry
around my inkpot or to run into the flames

to save my words as the rest of London burns.
For every painting in the Uffizi, I know

a thousand women with wild beating hearts
were lost, hung by the neck until dead.

So why am I writing this down?
Why bother writing at all?

annunciation II-IV

flandes 1519

I don't think he came to tell her she was having a baby.
Men may believe this is the greatest purpose in life—

to bring forth another man into this world—but angels,
especially the hermaphroditic Gabriel, must know better.

I imagine the news pertains to the book she is holding,
to the page trapped between her thumb and forefinger.

Gabriel stops her here, presses upon her
not as a single voice but as the loudest
of a growing multitude.

A passion, all consuming, eclipses her mind.
What she accepts is not the scepter of sainthood,
but a hunger. A pen.

allori 1578

You're holding your heart
as if it might fall out of you.

And the angels, despite their best
efforts with smiles

and patient gestures,
in waving the white lily, in singing,

in laughing, in the trumpeting of Heaven—
nothing will lift your gaze.

Nothing can turn you away
from the broken pen on the floor.

Forget what is coming.
You can see only what's lost.

Even as one hand turns up in resignation,
palm opening to accept the angel's song—

your foot is arching.
You ready yourself to run.

allori 1603

Why did you come back, Alessandro?
Did you forget something?

Why paint her twice and both instances
in such stark contrast. Here no heaven.

There's barely an angel and though Mary still
cannot look up from the floor,

I know this face, this plea for intervention.
If you'd given her but a few more inches,

a slighter bend in the elbows, she'd reach
right out for me. And Gabriel, too,

looks less willing to play the messenger,
more apologetic for interrupting

the last book she'll read with abandon.
What has happened to him these past 25 years,

to give him awareness, compassion
for the young girl whose life would forever

be cleaved in two by his coming? *Before. After.*
What happened to him? What happened to you?

the convent of san marco

Could you imagine that in *this* cloister, in *this* room,
a woman in man's clothing,

and a homosexual no less, would walk your little corridors?
That she would press her face in on your paintings?

Note how the doors arched, how the windows
covered in wood, opened?

It's been six hundred years, but could you bear it?
Her audacity to look down at the Annunciation,

to scrutinize the embellishments of your illuminated
manuscript. The size of your small room.

Did you ever picture her there?
As you sat at your desk, alone,

as the candle flame parried with the long shadows
on the wall, did you hear her footfall in the hallway?

A soft knocking at your door?
And if so—would you have let her in?

ode to a fellow writer in notebooks

Forgive my assumptions but I see you
have a notebook, red leather

to complement the gray of mine.
And a black ink pen, professing seriousness

to the way you're approaching this.
I can't help but notice as you wander

the galleries and look up into the oiled
canvases, you pause longest on each face,

on each palm, before looking away
as if ashamed. We pause

at the same paintings, and when
our eyes meet, though momentary,

it feels as if I'm passing a mirror,
a quick reflection of the me I never see.

Before I move on again, I must ask:
what do you hope to find here?

What is there to gain? Maybe we can
answer your questions as well as mine.

> the young martyr
> paul delaroche

What is in the water?

> A halo?
> An upturned crown?

—and the man on the shore,
> on horseback—

is he waving?

> yelling?
> bidding her farewell?

It's hard to tell in the darkness
> who is friend,
> who is foe,

and whether the hands,
> bound loosely in front,
> might have been her own doing.

little medieval boxes
france xv

I wonder what was kept inside
and for whom—though I suspect a *her*
given the hexagonal petals spread wide
and maybe a child, with the comical
triangular faces like elongated Jack
o' Lanterns. Or perhaps you were a child
when it was given to you, but then
you grew up. The lock is broken.
By you? By a suspicious lover or father?
And again, what was kept inside?
Letters? Your dowry? Your mother's
handkerchief or a small ring? Dried flowers
from a perfect afternoon in a lavender field?
Or a book? Written by you or another?
If nothing else, certainly
it's large enough to house a human heart—
and the little box beside it, a soul.

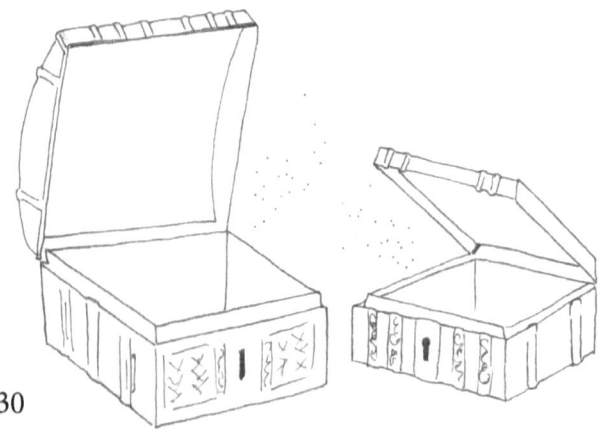

parable of the lost
domenico fetti

Sometimes when I cannot sleep
at night I light a candle.

I ignore the overturned chair but cannot
as easily dismiss the long shadows

cast against the wall,
the fervid dance of loss.

The light is the cause of all my misery.
Had I not first the flame,

there would be no shadow,
no requirement to embrace the dark,

no need to look down into the deep
and see what is left of me.

joan of arc
jules eugene lenepveu

You look frightened, but in a tolerable way.
The way babies will smile just before
their lips tremble, cheeks crumbling to a wail.

In the way your foot stops, mid-step,
the delicate arch exposed and bare.
Behind you, life continues—

The sounds of mewling sheep, grass ripping
free, and your mother at work, crouched
with fruit in one hand, a knife in the other.

Your heart must've beat hard
in the midst of all this transformation.
This moment between one life and the next.

Did you know God might call?
After all, your shoulder bag is packed.
Your hand is already lifting to accept the sword

offered. But the voice—how did you know it
when it came in its ethereal blue,
sudden and soft at the nape of your neck.

How did you recognize it for *good*?
So often I mistake it for the other voice,
the dark one, who would lead me astray.

                                        the artist's studio
                                        gustave courbert

At least you can see the faces.
You know who crowds your table.

For me, it's less clear cut.
The influence, they have no names,

but it's true they press in from the right
like a sun, warming the page.

And from the left, cold expectations
and the needs of a world rising,

like a tsunami wave to wash over me.
My hands freeze in such cold waters,

& even if I find the pen again,
I often cannot bring myself to hold it.

I admire your acknowledgment
of how many people come into the room

and sit down beside the artist.
But someone is missing, Courbert.

Not the patrons, commentators,
not your proud self,

nor even the world you draw upon.
You've forgotten the one

who stands thick and misshapen
in the corner. The one whose hunger,

whose presence, is always felt. The
phantom watching, waiting to see you fail.

                              ode to the unnamed
                              mummy in the louvre

Who were you, misshapen one?
And if names mean nothing
then what did you do?

Were you a cat-worshipping
seamstress? I've known a few.
Or someone less fortunate, your power

exhibited only over the act
of emptying another's chamber pot?
Excuse me for assuming a certain

station in life, but you've no gold
coffin. No blue stone scarab pinned
to your breast. You have nothing

to suggest you lived
in service of yourself, rather than
another. But even with queens

a life can be spent
in the shadow of a husband. Was yours,
maybe, a sensitive scribe?

Did he give his days to the dark tunnels
of someone else's tomb, carving
his own legacy, and leaving you

to wash out someone else's toilet?
Maybe you lived all of these lives—
and more. I wouldn't blame you,

if after such a man, a life, you vowed
to be done with the whole business
of art, done with self-deluded poets

who leave the hard work of living
to everyone else. Fools, all of them,
who won't hesitate to take

what they want of anyone, of you,
and butcher it. Even your stories,
the one thing best told by yourself.

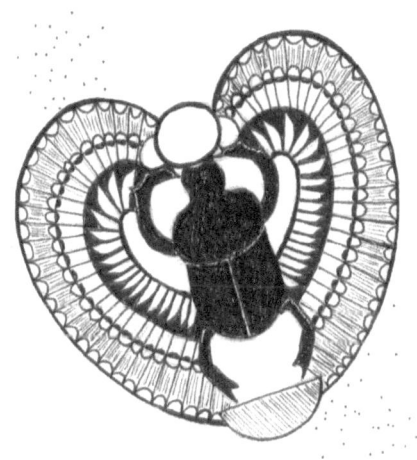

II.

> the seasons
> giuseppe arcimboldo

Because a woman is never just a woman,
but rather what each season has made of her.

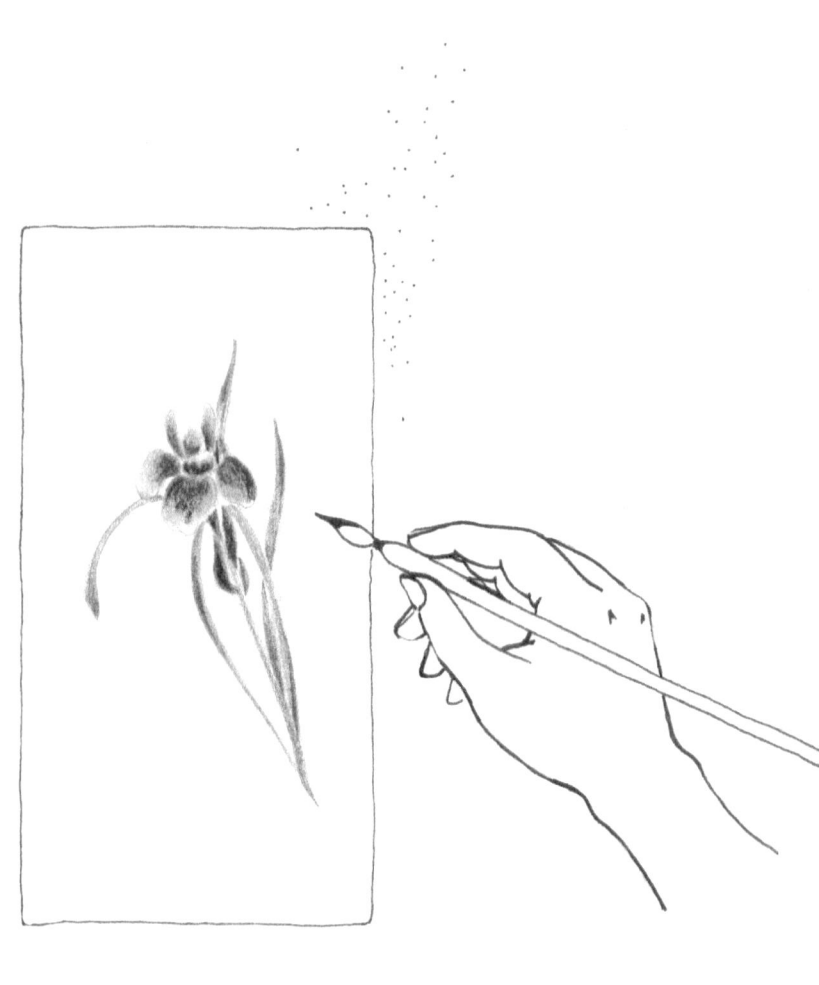

6 beauties from the pleasure quarter
chōbunsai eishi

To the right a flower, to the left a name
of the courtesan pictured there. The same
is true of each panel, the six connected
by flower and name and repeating objects.
Their arts: dancing, calligraphy, ikebana, haiku,
even their tea ceremonies, gesture perfect.

They made their own furniture and costumes.
Did she make this red-lacquered table, the plumes
with peacock feathers or the erupting blossoms cherry-
white? The diaphanous black kimono its own verse.
A woman whose art is for display only, is so very—

I can think of nothing worse.

The narrow sash is meant to convey grace,
demure, as her hair is pulled up away from her face.
But look at the way she holds her pen, how she leans
her cheek into the soft flesh of a palm. What is seen
in her half-closed eyes? In the folds of a white sash?
Morokoshi sits and reads, books complete with

bookmarks—indicative of a many-sided education. This
is my proof. That tousled stack my once grievance:
if she has learned, she knows. In her blossom-viewing
parties, repetitive summons to a boisterous tea-brewing

house, in her walks under lighted paper lanterns and
star-drunk nights—in all of it, she has seen something of

the world, felt the smallness of her place in it. And wept.
But what do I know of a servant girl from Kyoto?
Can I properly imagine the dissatisfaction, the pit, a hunger
in such a girl's stomach, of how it might ruin her?
What it means for a body to hollow and fill again,
insatiable with black fire. And then there's the mind—

still reaching for something, the crux of a hand unfilled.

                              the beggars
                              pieter bruegel

Beggars like artists come
from a long line, a tradition not corporeal
as much as compulsive. One day you wake up
and find yourself on the street,
hand opening to the passerby.
One night you reach for a pen and then
you can't remember what you picked it up for,
like entering a room only to find Purpose
unable to cross the threshold with you—
You wait, uncertain, on the other side
until it finds you again. Does it comfort you
to know my words are as unsteady as your hand?
What is so threatening about a palm,
bare and vulnerable in the light?
Why should my chest hurt as I measure the steps
between where I leave you and where I'm going?
Perhaps it's simply difficult to watch
another asking for the same answers.

the raft of medusa
theodore gericault

Gericault knew what he was doing
when he put the boat in the distance,
on the horizon, because what else

could they reach for?
Those reaching tore at each other's
skin and hair. Only two men were

able to wave their own shirts
while their brethren clutched nothing
but bare backs, and the raft

keeping them afloat. One pulls
at another, and the shadows make it
difficult to say if it is love or hate

in each embrace. Only one—
the eldest—has given up,
his face turned away from the horizon.

He's the wisest, I'd say.
So often it's impossible to know
if salvation is coming or going.

on stone

minnakht, chief priest of akhmim

I relied on the stone. I thought
it would ensure eternity

for my work. With it, even
the worthless (majority) might survive.

But the revisions! The loss of flesh
around the fingers by a misplaced chisel.

The rejections were slower in coming.
You take down the wall! I'd say.

And those so quick to criticize
did not commit to the labor. But I could

do nothing about the students—
or the gods forbid—

others equipped with their own tools,
who felt compelled to go around hacking.

(For most) You don't need to understand it
to take a swing. Like a green-winged scarab,

nothing can stop us from pushing
our shit across the floor.

And let's be honest:
In this way, I am no better.

the dance of zalongo
ary scheffer

She prays, her hands high. One shining eye does not waver.
It's not faith, this desperation.
The eye is too wide and the lips too far apart

as a golden child clutches her knees. You would think
they should do more to cloak themselves.
Bare breasts everywhere, and muscular backs

will surely excite the soldiers, the blazing fire on the hill.
One covers her head, a mother bent, but
the infant is still screaming. Others beat their chests,

pull at their hair. It's clear they're still fighting.
They still have hope. Except for one, resigned,
her face and her heart dark. This one knows what's coming.

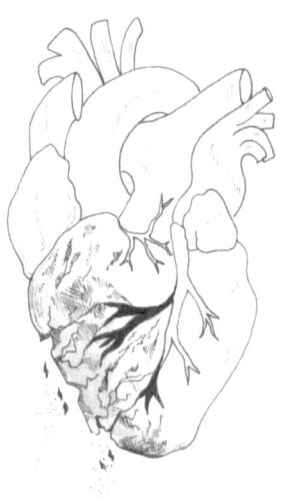

the coronation
jacques-louis david

The moment of triumph, in placing
his crown upon his own head,
in declaring his agency.

The painter forgot nothing, including
even the bored choir boy, dragging
his incense along the floor.

The gilded ladies
in matching gowns,
each channeled a unique emotion.

This one jealousy.
That one the weight of duty.
And the last—envy of a man's power.

But it's the painting I'm not looking at
that strikes me more. Not the sculpted
saints in Sully's Notre Dame. No. But

Napoleon handsome in his gray suit,
on his tired horse. Napoleon
in the dead of winter,

passing through the mountain's shadow.
My mind turns always
toward the inevitable fall.

the burning of troy
stefano della bella

Why must everything built, one day
come down? The screaming
reverberates against unyielding stone

walls. Sometimes a whole city is
swallowed by a starved sea.
A man's throat is split

open suddenly in the dark,
like a rare red blossom, while
torchlight dances victorious in his eyes.

These moments breathe like dreams.
The flame hypnotic. Hellish
as if Hades itself had erupted through

the soil, opening its great mouth
beneath all of you.
Horses flying past mistaken for hounds.

The white smoke of their souls
are rising, cold in the night.
Ashes from the pyre.

Death, when distant,
can also be beautiful. Especially
when we pretend it isn't real.

in the tomb of donatello

It's not a dream. You're dead.
But don't worry.

No love like Medici love,
my friend. I love you so much

I'll build a tomb for you,
nearest my own,

so that when we're both dead
I can ask you everything

about your work, your inspiration,
the real meaning behind

the way that bronze
boy's hat juts, the quirk of a smile

on his fixed face. I can ask
what was it was like

to have your hands around each
figure as you drew them to life,

like an alchemist, pulling them free
of the sorcerer's stone.

I'll ask so many questions
because we're dead

and without distraction
and because I'll have no one else

to talk to and no one
to remember me for the Florentine

prince that I was. Once
you have enough of me, you'll yell.

Beg me to be silent.
Can't a man get rest even in his own grave?

For six hundred years, I'll oblige you.
Until one day a tourist will stop by,

press her little pig nose in on us,
and step right over your body

as if it isn't even there.
Who is she? you'll ask, surprised.

Or maybe, *why do they keep coming
here? They'll have their own soon enough.*

Then at last, I'll have the chance to ask:
Who is that speaking in the darkness?

michelangelo's tomb

Three beautiful women ready to serve you even in death.
Painting, Sculpture, Architecture,
did you imagine them this way? As women,

with muscle-pulling bone as they slid into your room,
and crept up behind you. As a sudden warm hand
laid over yours. Did they whisper in the dark hours

between one creation and the next? In the dark
before you could fall asleep? A soft finger rubbing
the skin between your brows.

Did these voices keep you awake at night?
Or could you not sleep until you heard them come
in and lay down beside you?

And how about now? Are their hands still soft,
voices gentle? Praise abundant?
Or have they grown teeth in the after?

                    hercules fighting the centaurs
                              pietro benvenuti

Why would you idealize that, the victor
wearing his half-beast brother like a skin?
Why should men be strong only because
they've made slaves of another, of the natural?

The centaur cradles a vase. The man thrusts a
sword. I'm not confused as to who is civilized here.
Pietro, would you still make him this way?
Name him Hercules, enslaver of beasts,

if you could see us now, with our factory farms,
our razed, blackened lands, our filthy seas.
Would you call this victory?
Would you still call us *man*?

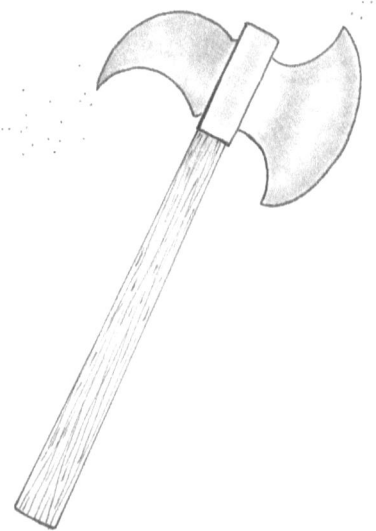

                              the sacrifice
                              stefano pieri

Who was really testing who here?
And how did the goat get brought into this?
I think it angers me most—the bowed head,
the stoic way the horns are bent,
not in defense, but resignation
as the beast comes up the hill. As he prepares
to lay down in those thickets so
Isaac can be spared.
When did the goat become the responsible party,
the willing to inherit all the sins of the earth?
Why should Nature wait while we blunder
as alcoholics stumbling in the dark,
the codependent child lifting us again
into our own bed? Paint me something
bucolic next time, would you? Paint Isaac, alive,
as the steward, tending his flock
on a lush summer hill. Something pleasant
because I need no reminder of you.

                              judith and her maid servant
                                      artemisia gentileschi

Judith turns as if in a dream, her eyes
only half open in waking.
And the sword, propped against one shoulder—
can she even feel it? The weight of it,
of the severed head in the basket—
the weight of what she has done?

What have you done, Artemisia, with
the weight of your paintbrush
cramping your fingers? When your eyes
at last fluttered open and you found a
painting before you, were you
surprised to see it? Or was it more or less intact,
resembling the faces from your dreams?

Or maybe you were saddened by the sight
as I often am when I see my half-breathing creation,
my failed birth, wet & malformed in my hands.

It leaves you cold, doesn't it? Like
a sudden extinguished flame. Without the smoke
one would never have known the spirit of inspiration
had come at all. Without the heat
I always forget there was once a flame.

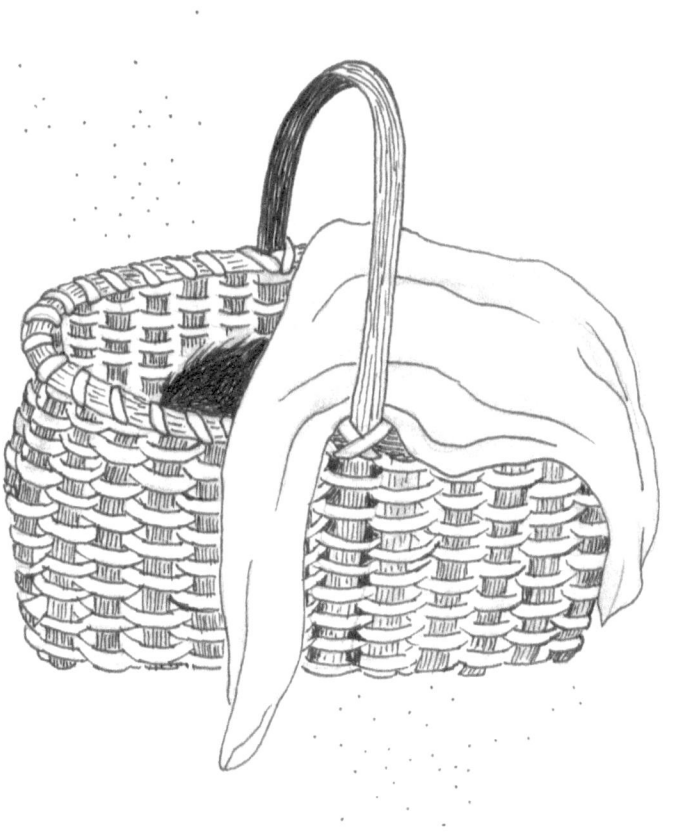

                                    the battlefield of eylau
                                    antoine-jean gros

Everyone watches him,
even those dying.

Napoleon's gaze remains
on the invisible, the distance.
His hand outstretched for
something the rest cannot see.

How does he do it?

Ignore the fearful whine
of his horse, the screams
of his dying men?

The sound of cut throats
gurgling, choking on
the words that won't come?

In moments such as these,
I can never manage
to reassemble my mind,

or my heart. The whole world
rides me like that whipped horse.

Perhaps Napoleon had only one
choice: keep his eyes firm
on dawn's horizon—or die.

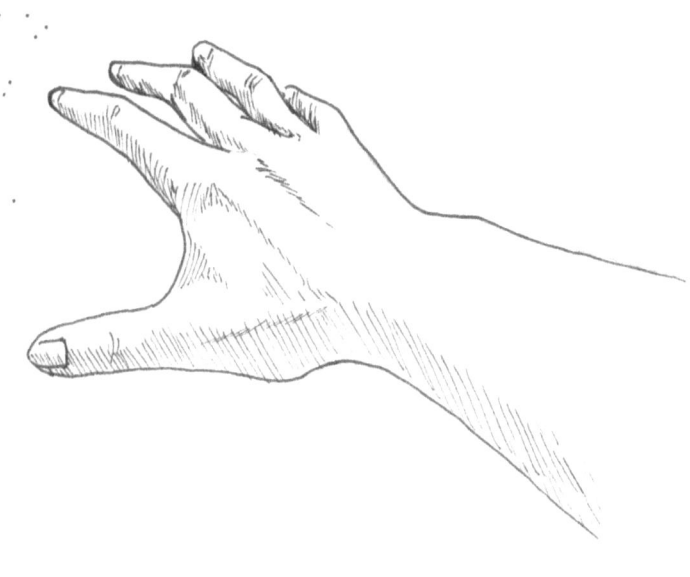

III.

> the medici chapels
> michelangelo

All that you loved was dead
or dying, and you, suspended
high above the stone floor.

What is it that saved you?
The paintbrush in your hand?
Never looking down?

The terrible vision of your brains
all over the floor, your body busted
at your friends' feet? Perhaps

it was the drive of a final task. Leave
homage to those you love before
you yourself are burned to smoke.

Did you know as you hung there
above their marble tombs, it was just
a matter of letting go?

Leaning back and letting
the world take what it wanted of you?
Or did you know the only chance

of immortality for yourself,
for those you love, cold at your feet,

was to preserve this moment, suspend

it in stasis, like Selene, who would
rather see her lover sleep at the brink
of death than disperse into oblivion?

Did you make this choice consciously
not to go down, not to yield to the
marble as it so often yielded to you?

Did you choose instead to give yourself
piece by piece to the ravenous world,
hoping something of you might survive?

mary magdalene
artemisia gentileschi

Again I think of the woman, the artist,
and not the painting. The way your hand
must have moved over the canvas
or the way your eyes must have wandered
as you mixed the paints. To what? To whom?
Toward the window to inspect the light?
Toward a question asked from the doorway?
Did you pause at the edge of your subject's
mouth, or at the corner of the eye
before touching the canvas each time?
Did you see possibility or accusation, when
confronted with a blank canvas?
Did you brace yourself, your subject,
against a world where women were nothing?
Did you worry it would always be this way?
Servitude, children, and husbands with too
many debts? What did the *first* stroke feel like?
The last? Was it a swell of pride or defeat
that overtook you as you leaned the result
against the wall to dry, inspecting every blemish
with a dragon's eye? I know the feeling
of spreading myself out to see how thin
I can make me before greater forces win.
Is that what happened here? Or—
did you simply relax your fingers and let go?

questions for the dead
bas-reliefs from the temple of satet at elephantine

Someone did this to the stone,
took nothing and carved

an inviting curvature.
Traced with a loving hand, a mesmerized

finger. Someone cut
each mark of the face drawn.

The distinctive nose, perhaps
their own, now immortalized forever

& the snake curling around the cup—
did you do this?

Tell me what it means & if you knew
it would survive four thousand years.

If you didn't know, your inscriptions
were excavated, carefully lifted

from Egyptian soil, the balmy sap
of the Nile now one with the stone.

I'm sorry to tell you that the tomb
where you labored for many nights,

hunchbacked, crumbled to dust.
Which mattered more to you?

The work or the place?
Or the life where both were encased?

Now your words are displayed, observed
by hundreds of indifferent boyfriends,

& half-wit tourists sparing only a glance
before rushing on to find the Mona Lisa.

But they're here. They remain. Do you
lament the time you forfeited

to carve out this piece of eternity?
The blistered hands, the solitude spent
in the dark with only the sound
of your chisel chipping away all

that suffocated you?
Do I only ask these questions because

I'm alive? And therefore, foolish.
Does it matter how one's life is spent?

To the living, yes.
But what about to the dead?

emergence, ode to the unfinished work
unfinished michelangelo sculptures

1.

It is oddly comforting to see you this way.
Unpolished. Rough
edges give more reality than perfected stone.
In an aggregated edge of rock,
half a face is exposed, the curve of a jaw
above water. It begs the question
of what lies beneath. A realization.
There is a cold patina
of stone where you lovingly ran each hand,
waiting for their eyes to open.

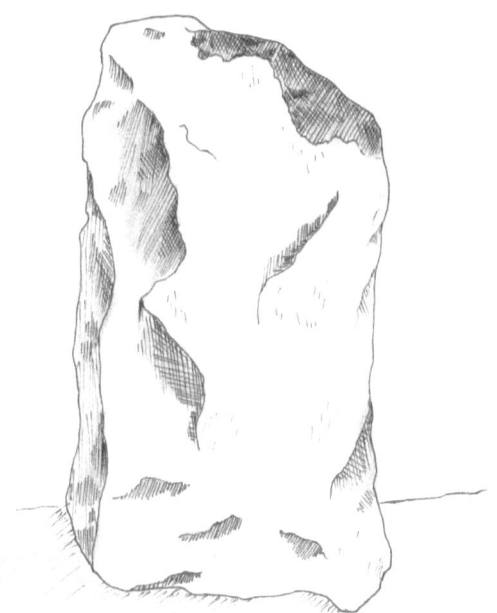

2.

Sculpting: maybe not like a story, crafted.

More like a poem, free flowing and alive.
And you just trying to capture enough
of it to establish a foothold in our reality.

In your mind's eye, the figures coursed
with movement or just the suggestion
of a shape flickering in water, a play of

shadow. Here they whispered
or seemed to—but were still so far away.

You strain to hear them better,
to bring forth a body, like Frankenstein,
immortal and hardy enough to house
one of your darkest secrets.

But these stone bodies are incomplete.
                    Why?
        Why did they refuse you?
Why did they pull deeper into the sediment
        burrowing into the soil faster than you
could unbury them?

Or did you gladly stop?

As you held its body in your hand, did it move
serpentine between your muscular palms?

Did a great, yellow draconian eye open
and fix upon you? Did you realize
in a breathless moment what you were creating?

Did you have the foresight to let the demon lie?

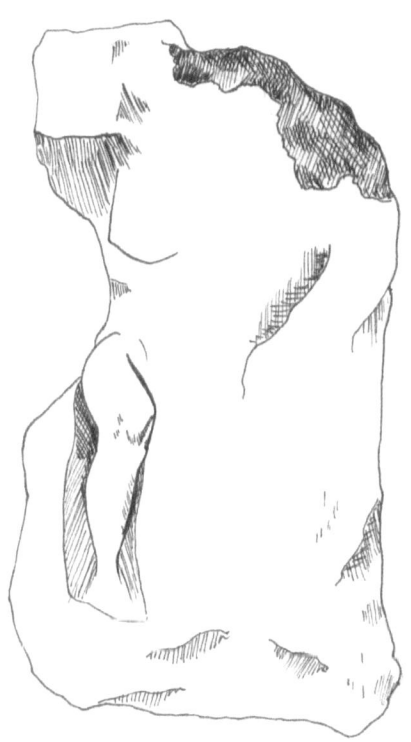

3.

I'm most interested in the other world.
The one I can feel,

like a pulse throbbing, somewhere
just behind the eyes.

I can almost see it, if I turn fast enough
and catch more than a flicker of light.

I haven't succeeded yet. But like any
foolhardy soul, I'll keep trying.

In these other worlds, I'm sure life, or unlife,
courses just as varied and ambiguous as our own.

Even if they're not as light dependent as we are,
they must orbit something.

A species, after cropping up, must evolve
and rely on the patience of benevolent gods,

as it stumbles blindly into adulthood,
a world deemed "other" connecting to *this* world.

Semantics aside, I picture it,
like a Rubik's cube, rotating. Where

do the connections align? What center point
connects all of the moving pieces?

I cannot see it clearly from here.
But I feel it enacting its will upon my bones.
—and my mind.

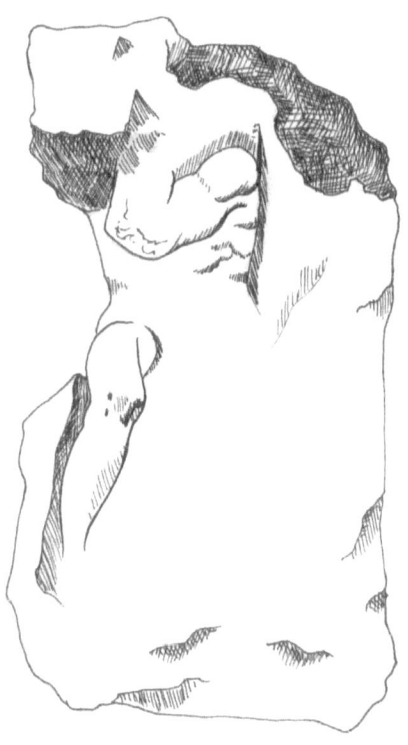

4.

With poor eyesight, it's difficult to draw
any conclusions. Even in the heart
low visibility refracts light.

      Depending on the day, the hour of the day,
the food consumed within the minutes of the hour—all
the world looks different. Variables make the world
prismatic. Angle is everything.

From this angle, I can only say something exists.

And like a gatekeeper, I note the separation dividing *here*
from *there*. I know I must keep my post. I must be
careful of what I let into this world.

Like any invasive species,
the smallest of seeds can germinate, propagate
without limit. More voracious than any Napoleonic desire.

More importantly, if one is not careful
if one does not discern what is emerging from stone,
from a story, from a heart…

Let's just say it was probably for the best
that you laid down your chisel on that day.

That the prism turned and changed the light.
That a lover asked for a kiss.
That a ceiling needed to be painted.

It was probably for the best.

    May it always be for the best.

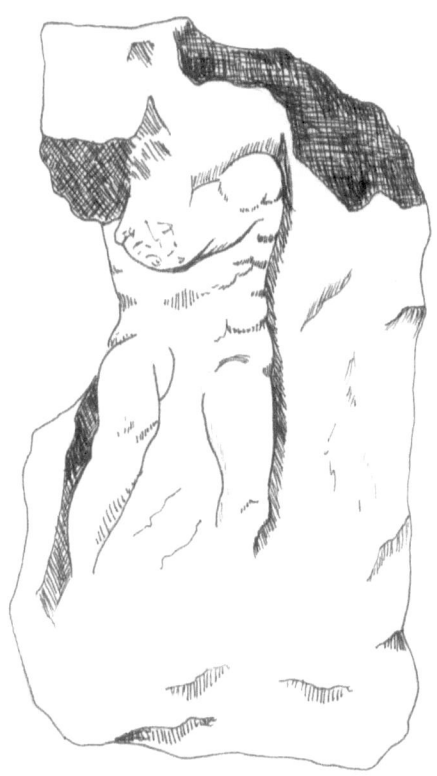

hercules at the crossroads
pietro benvenuti

And that's the truth, isn't it?

When you most need something
done—some pressing task heavy
on your heart—all of the world
welcomes you. A wave of smiling faces

swells up to drag you down
into soft arms. The fragrant laughter
hanging even from the trees, red and ripe,
and the music as sweet as a mother's hymn.

Or worse, everything goes wrong. Things
that never require attention, need attention.

In either case, thank the gods for a friend
who holds a shield over your head
to block out the sun weakening you
into complacency.

Thank the gods for the smallest of voices,
for wings spread on either side,
and calves flexed in the ready.
The patient hand still pointing the way.

a final question

The cat at San Lorenzo basilica is not thin.
The arch of its tortoise-shell back,
the way its rump spreads wide when
it lays itself down in the Tuscan sun—
both suggest life is good
in the courtyard beneath the *albero arancione*.
All of the ledges, hedges, and cobblestone
walks must provide amusement & seclusion
from the tourists gawking
at ancient relics, from the recession,
from Bellacosi, and American girls
with notebooks. Here, each afternoon,
the cat is free
to gather the remains of February's heat
into its soft fur. Can one ever ask for more
than a patch of sun to warm the coldest day?

transmutation

Enough, or it should be, to know death
is not the end. Oxygen
existed before combining with hydrogen
to become water, before evaporating
into a great blue atmosphere.
Matter existed even in the hollow of space,
before it spun itself into a planetary system,
forming one rock just the right distance
from the sun to breed life. And then
like all successful experiments,
get out of hand. It should be enough
to know that when you are finished
with this body, you will be *some*thing,
*some*where—though how much
of the sky is still the sea drop,
it's hard to say. But you'll be here—
as a sunbeam on a blank page.
As a C# struck by a clumsy finger. As
smoke rising from an extinguished flame.

les nymphéas
monet

1.

Soft detail

because there is something that cannot be
captured in paint (or words),
lost in the passage

between the ethereal and the physical.
You understood the disservice to beauty
to use sharp lines,
to boast of definitions—the audacity.

Your garden was merely the glove,
lace stretched over a hand
made alive by Nature's breathing.
And your painting—nothing

more than afternoon light across her cheek.

2.

Use water to suggest depth and the place
where the lily pads touch beneath.
You touch the verdant expanse

and find a cartographer's dilemma.
You want us to see
the door between *here* and *there*,

the point where lovers' palms kiss,
somehow coming together,
despite the infinity of space expanding

between them.
Matter is mostly space between atoms.
Art is mostly space between craft

and intuition. A navigation
done in complete darkness.
We know the arrival when we see it,

but the getting there is blind.
For me, it's often recognized as a warm
heat spreading in the chest. It glows

until the embers are bright enough
to illuminate a seam. A way in. A door
revealed as a single green pad floating

on top of an invisible air pocket.
Your painting is a kindness, holding
space between your worlds and mine.

3.

Water and light as travelers
dance between
this world and the next. As conduits

they're best examined with a soft gaze
because *the closer you look the less you'll see*
of the world that presses against you

in the quietest of hours, translations
that you didn't expect—nor fully comprehend—
come. As light through a water glass, as

a gray shadow in wet eyes, illuminated
by candlelight so sudden you find your hand
is lifting to take hold of it—

lifting as if possessed
and by what you dare not ask, knowing the real
danger lies only in holding the brush too tight.

4.

We are still in the water because
part of you must be submerged.
Pulling up art is like pulling up rice.

You can't see what's down there,
what you're grabbing onto it, but
with practice, you'll know it by touch.

Still, we have all the problems
with translation—the infinite ways
language can fail us. It's a crude habit

of clasping a collar
on what must be free to move.
Unless free, how can it demonstrate

the prowess that first amazed you?
This is why you never paint below
the surface of the pond.

That isn't the translation you're after.
Like a seamstress turning the cloth
over and over in her hands,

you can see the dress. The parasol
opening. You know where you're going,
but not where you've been.

You can't imagine the field of cotton,
sunlight brightening the cloud-like fibers,
or the fingers that bled when picking it.

You only know your own position
in the assembly line, where to place
the next stitch, the brush.

Accept this small gift of forever.

portrait of mrs. pagliano bruno
edoardo gelli

The shoes she wears were cobbled by someone's hands.
The hat on her head threaded
for a reason we will never know,
by a face we will never see in a place—

a dark basement,
or bright kitchen,
beneath the window of a dim shop—some*where*
we will never stumble across when turning down

roads populated with the ghosts
of those who laid them, and those who erected the streetlamps,
the stones squaring off the little offices
where strained backs bent over little designs,

by candlelight made possible because the wax was dipped,
by hands belonging to a body. Even as those before us
imagined more ways to bring light into the world,
the rest of us were busy forgetting the people in it.

Even before that, people rode horses through fields
that had never seen people, carrying carefully marked maps
that would only later be washed unfinished downstream,
so that another, dressing differently,

can transverse the same land.
Mark it all down again. Get the credit.
What is one man's loss is another's reputation
and so on until—Infinite probabilities coalesced and
"I" came to be

standing in a room, in Florence, which was not always Florence,
encased in stone walls placed by dead hands upon the ground.
A palace that is no longer a palace and paintings
immortalizing the suggestion of a face long since
rendered to dust.

Skulls lying in some grave that others have forgotten,
and may pass by without knowing who they are looking at.
This painting, though beautiful, will be lost in a flood, a
fire, a storm—
give or take a million years.

We have lost the midwives, the seamstresses of our world,
those who turn the fabric over in their hands,
folding this dimension to the next and stitching it
into something worth seeing, smelling, tasting,

feeling against one's skin. A chair for a sore back, a pillow
for one's heavy head, giving us the next best thing
before passing into oblivion themselves.
Forgotten. Nameless—

but not lost.
Because here I am laying my easel over yours.
Here I am picking up where you left off,
for better or worse—

in obscurity, yes, but not alone.
As you borrowed all of your utensils, so have I.
Your sky.
Your light.

I take everything that was yours, knowing
it is only for a matter of time
before the world takes everything from me—

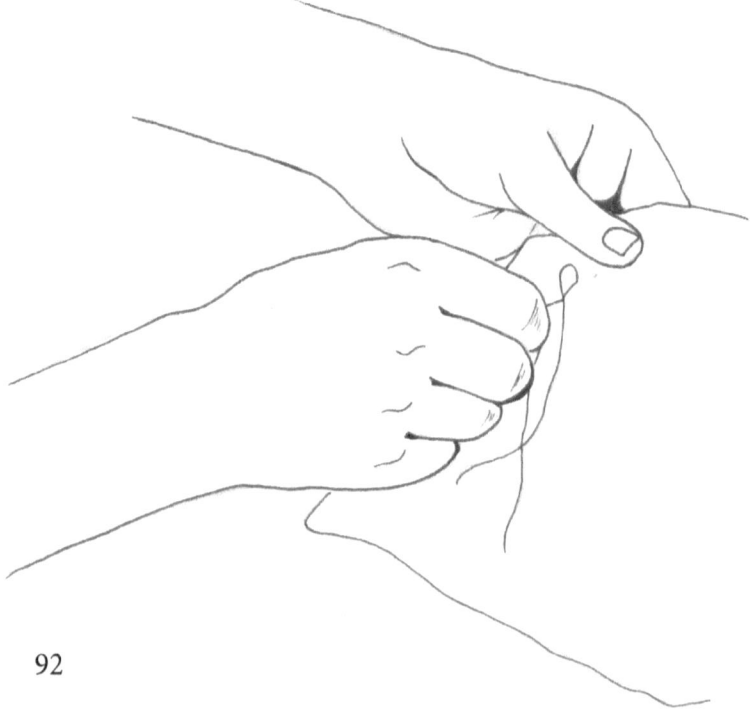

author's note

Dear reader,

I hope you enjoyed this collection. If you would be so kind, please leave a review for it on whichever retail sites you prefer.

It would mean so much to me, and to the other poetry lovers who may discover this collection because of your review. Not to mention reviews are one of the best ways to support the writers and artists you love.

If you want more poems, you can visit me at
https://www.korymshrum.com/free-starter-library

For more art from the amazing, Victoria Solomon, you can follow her on Instagram @victoriamsolomon

On my website, you can also sign up for my newsletter and receive a free poetry chapbook. The newsletter will be sent 2-3 times a month and contain free poems and updates about my work. I will never share your email and, of course, you can unsubscribe at any time.

Hope to chat with you soon!

k.b. marie

also by k.b. marie

birds & other dreamers

questions for the dead

you can't keep it

about the author

K.B. Marie has published over thirty poems in magazines such as *Bateau, North American Review, Ascent*, and elsewhere under the name, Kory M. Shrum. She earned her MFA at Western Michigan University and has worked for *New Issues Press*, *Zone 3 Press*, and *Third Coast Literary Magazine*.

For ten years, she taught writing to thousands of university students before deciding to write full-time. Her favorite kind of poetry combines art and words – which is why her work is often accompanied with illustrations or other visuals.

She lives in Michigan with her equally well-read wife, Kimberly, and their rescue pug, Charley.

Anything else you'd like to know can be found at https://www.korymshrum.com/poetry

about the illustrator

Victoria Solomon is a Michigan-based artist specializing in pencil and ink portraiture and other art. When not powering through nursing school, she loves to experiment with new art supplies and write fiction. She also makes an incredible chocolate cake. Victoria shares her home with her husband and her small brood of children and cats.

Follow her on Instagram @victoriamsolomon

www.ingramcontent.com/pod-product-compliance
Lightning Source LLC
Chambersburg PA
CBHW030158100526
44592CB00009B/335